The Soul's Calendar

Rudolf Steiner

A new translation

Adrian Anderson

Pocket Edition

www.rudolfsteinerstudies.com

Threshold Publishing, Australia

Distributed by:
Ebook Alchemy
Prahran VIC 3181

ISBN 978-0-6481358-7-6

"Humanity must again learn to be able to think of the Spiritual as connected to the natural yearly cycle. Today the power must awaken to directly link the sensory appearance of the world, with the Spirit."

(Rudolf Steiner   lecture, April 1, 1923, GA 223)

"Our inner {soul} processes, are now less connected to time, to the cycle of the year, but if we bring our own 'timeless' soul activity into correspondence with the temporal rhythms of the year, then great secrets of existence will unfold for us. The year becomes the great archetype of humankind's own soul processes, and thereby a fruitful source of self-knowledge."

(Rudolf Steiner, Introduction to *The Soul's Calendar,* 1912)

Contents:

Introduction: the variable 'Easter' date, the 2 sequences built into the verses, and the unauthorized changes to the first edition, of 1912.

Verses 1 - 52: German texts and English translation

Appendix 1: Verses corrected because of the unauthorized changes

Appendix 2: Glossary of some key terms

A Pocket Edition

This pocket edition is designed to be taken in your pocket whenever you are out and about, so whenever a moment presents itself, you can look at the scenes around you, and bring the verse to mind. This is a wonderful way to train one's soul to become sensitive to the presence of the spiritual behind the physical world. As each week goes by, different astral-etheric energies become present in the environment. Also the two other verses which mirror a polar opposite dynamic to each week, can be reflected on.

The system of numbers and letters included by Rudolf Steiner for this purpose are clearly shown.

For more about these topics, see the Annotated Commentary edition.

Introduction

Deeply attracted by the spiritual view of ecology embodied in The Soul's Calendar, I began to translate the verses in 1973, re-working my translations over several decades, as I experienced ever more deeply how these verses are a guide to the 'mood' of each week of the seasonal cycle of the hemisphere. These moods derive from the changing spiritual energies active in the Earth, in either hemisphere. The influences are present in the aura of our planet, and they also stream into the hemisphere from the cosmos.

Rudolf Steiner uses the term, 'the Earth-soul' to mean our planet as a living organism, with life-forces and with many 'ensouled' beings (humans and animals, and also a range of deities, and lesser nature spirits).

Above some key verses, Rudolf Steiner put a number of headings, to identify the season it belonged to, thereby confirming for us that the verses follow a hemisphere's seasonal cycle, as these are not abstract 'global' verses. The hemispherical basis was also confirmed in July 1923. At that time a student, who had lived in South America, questioned him about The Soul's Calendar with regard to the southern hemisphere. The student was told to reverse the cycle of the verses so they begin in the springtime of that hemisphere.[1]

This advice in turn means that the 'Easter' verse does not refer to the church festival. Here 'Easter' refers to the first Sunday after the first Full Moon after the spring equinox of **either** hemisphere, when the 'new year' actually begins. So, 'Easter' refers to the springtime, as the natural start of the New Year. The word 'Easter' is derived from 'Eostre', a Celtic word for the springtime and dawn of a new year.

The Soul's Calendar is a guidebook helping the soul to become sensitive to the spiritual realities active in the seasons.

---

[1] Fred Poeppig, reported in his *Abenteuer meines Lebens*, Novalis Verlag, 1975.

Rudolf Steiner indicated that from such awareness, a new cycle of festivals could be created – a cycle which is seasonal, but which also has an 'esoteric' Christian aspect.[2] Verse One was given two headings by Rudolf Steiner; 'Spring' and also the 'Easter Mood'.

The variable 'Easter' date:
Because of the variations of the Moon's cycles with regard to the solar year, verse 1 (the 'Easter' or Eostre verse) has a variable starting time, from year to year. For the southern hemisphere, it occurs between late September and late October. For the north, it occurs between late March and late April. If Verse 1 starts late, the length of the days allotted to each verse, leading up the summer solstice need to be shortened to about 5 days each.

But if Verse 1 starts early, the weeks are lengthened. Also, before this first verse of the New Year, if Easter is coming late, the number of days for verses 51 and 52 (i.e.,

---

[2] See the author's *Living a Spiritual Year* for a comprehensive study of this topic.

the time from the spring equinox up to Easter/Eostre), have to be increased, or if it comes early, they need to be shortened. So, living with The Soul's Calendar makes you more aware of the natural life-cycles of your own hemisphere, not only as the expression of biological processes, but also of spiritual realities.

Note: Those headings which are not from me, but are in Rudolf Steiner's original 1912 Soul's Calendar are in *this style of font*.

Two sequences built into the 52 verses.

Two 'mirroring' sequences have been interwoven. One of these sequences could be called 'the world within', and the other, 'the world without'.

The **'world-without' sequence** points out the differing dynamics between the hemisphere and the sun, but as felt by us. This sequence is marked out by the use of a **letter** given to each verse. Halfway through the book, the alphabet occurs again, but now with a bar over each letter. In this sequence, the year is a cycle which starts on verse A, the Easter-Eostre (spring) day, as a 'new year' day. This cycle dies away in the autumn. Then it starts up again with verse 'A bar' which mirrors verse A; and verse 'B bar' mirrors verse B, and so on, throughout the alphabet. See the following diagrams about these cycles.

Note that in the two sequences of letters, there is no letter 'j', because this letter has no formal place in the German alphabet. (Historically, it is only a variation of 'i', and hence it has no cosmic origin.)

The **world-within sequence** points to the difference for us of the spring-to-autumn phase, and the autumn-to-spring phase. In this sequence, each verse is numbered. The soul experiences the polarity, or mirroring effect, between verse 1 and verse 52, then verse 2 and 51, etc. This 'world-within' cycle is a more contemplative experience, whilst the 'world-without' sequence more directly reflects nature's processes, caused by the 'breathing-in' and 'breathing-out' processes, which each hemisphere undergoes during its spring and its autumn.

So in the 'world-within' cycle, the week of the New Year (Easter verse, no. 1) mirrors the week **just before** this, the last week of the old year, (verse 52). And as the verses move on to 2,3 and 4 etc, they are mirrored in their predecessors: 51,50 and 49, etc. The first half of this sequence (verses 1-26) could be thought of as '*the I in the cosmos*', whereas the second half (verses 27-52) could be thought of as '*the cosmos in the I*'.[3]

---

[3] To read more about these two sequences, see my *The Soul's Calendar: Annotated edition.*

1 **The world within:** contemplating the old year from the 'Eostre-born' New Year.

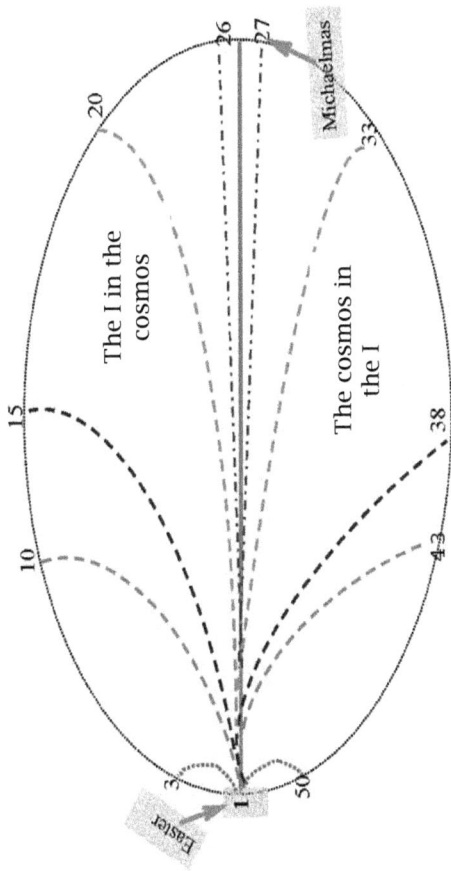

2 The world without: we feel the hemisphere's in- and out-breathing, harmonizing with the sun's motions.

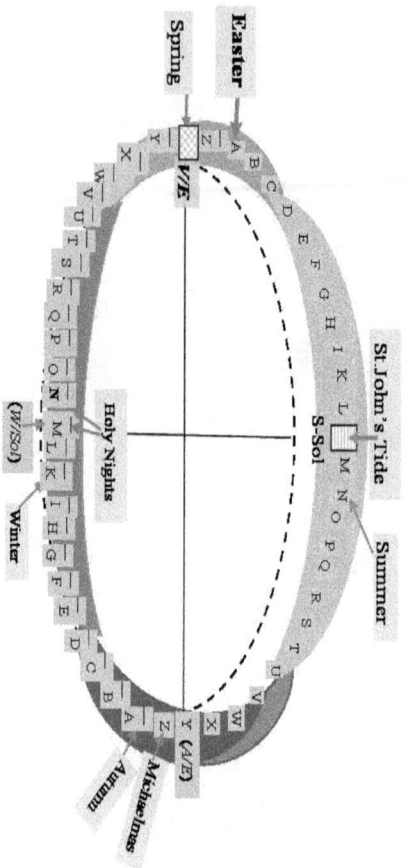

Alterations to Rudolf Steiner's original text

A recent document from the Rudolf Steiner Archives has revealed that some words written by Rudolf Steiner in his original manuscript were deleted and a different text was inserted.[1] This was done to nine verses in 1912, as the book was being prepared for publication. The Munich printer made these unauthorized changes, which have been incorporated ever since then, in all editions of the book. This happened because, for decades it was thought that Rudolf Steiner himself had made these changes.

But the editors in the Archives now know that these changes were made without authority from Rudolf Steiner. He was traveling when the printers were preparing his book, and could not be informed of these changes.

However, in 1918 Rudolf Steiner used this 1912 version, with its changes, for the eurythmy dance-forms. The Archive editors have recently suggested that this indicates that Rudolf Steiner found

---

[1] http://fvn-rsnet/indexphp.... Zur Textgestaltung des Seelenkalenders.

the changes to be acceptable. However, my conclusion is that he decided not to devote time and energy to correcting the alterations, as the book was now widely known, and above all, he was facing an extremely demanding situation.

For in 1918, Europe was convulsed by the catastrophes of the war; this was not the time to correct the 1912 error of judgement by the printers. In fact, such was the pressure he was under that, in writing out the text for the eurythmists in 1918, he made several mistakes, as the Archives note.

That Rudolf Steiner could not really be supportive of the unauthorized changes, can be seen in the fact that these changes distort or lessen the spiritual meaning of the relevant verses. And in some cases, the changed meanings are inconsistent with the underlying message of the verse.

These textual changes made in 1912 to these verses, are noted in this book, and the way they alter the message of the verse, are commented on briefly. The genuine original text from Rudolf Steiner was used for this edition. A note at the end of each relevant verse, advises the reader to see the Appendix for more information about the changes made to that verse. Further details about these changes are presented in my *The Soul's Calendar by Rudolf Steiner – Annotated Edition*.

Punctuation

The manuscript has very little punctuation, so the editors of the 1912 edition, and later editions, have quite correctly decided to add many commas and some other punctuation marks, to make the message of the verses clearer. However in a few cases, some additions or changes to the original punctuation has changed the actual focus of the verse; where this happened, I have pointed out the impact of such alterations.

It is also the case that the text for the book was written quickly, on hotel stationery, and apart from a few small errors, the manuscript also has a number of places where some words are crossed out and a different text is inserted, which conveys the meaning more clearly.

A Glossary of key terms
Included as an Appendix is a short list explaining some core anthroposophical terms used in the verses.

Blank Pages
To ensure that the German and English texts are facing each other there will be some blank pages.

Which week does a verse refer to?
There is the stable section of the verses; this is from the Summer Solstice day through to the Spring Equinox day. But there are also two variable sections of the year:
A: from the Spring Equinox day to the Easter/Eostre day,
B: from that day, through to the Summer Solstice day.
So approximate dates are included for all the verses, except for these two sections. These given dates are not meant to be taken as precise; they are a guide only,

because even they will vary by a few days each year. For example, even though this is the stable section of the year, and the verses normally start on a Sunday, the 'Summer Solstice' day, (i.e., the third day after the solstice) will often not fall on a Sunday. It is those variable sections (A & B) of the year which require specific attention. There is no value in giving set dates for those verses.

A further small problem is with the equivalent date for the 'Michaelmas' day and the Michaelmas verse, in the southern hemisphere. In the north it is Sept. 29th, not Sept. 25th (the natural day), due to an ancient visionary experience of the Archangel Michael having occurred on the 29th September.

A seasonal festival day always occurs 3 days after the solstices and equinoxes. In the south, to keep a similar link between the verses and the weeks, verse 26 could start on March 29th, instead of March 25th. As in the north, often that day will not be a Sunday.

Note: Writing in the dates of the variable verses

For verses of variable dates, i.e., verses 2 up to 11, and 51 & 52, a space is provided for you to write in the dates of each of those weeks, since their dates will vary greatly from year to year. (A pencil is recommended, so that each year, new dates can be written in.)
The space looks like this:

(Dates: -   )

Rudolf Steiner's German spelling system

The German text of the verses, as reproduced here, is that of Rudolf Steiner's hand-written manuscript. He used the German spelling prevailing at that time, which of course pre-dates the controversial 'new style', advocated in the 1990's. But his spelling system itself was replaced, in the 1912 book, with the 'Duden' system. This is a universally agreed font and spelling system developed by the printing trade, regardless of whether the author was Austrian or from southern or northern

Germany. The Archives, in their 1961 official version of this book, also used a form of the Duden system.

Verse 1 German

Oster-Stimmung

FRÜHLING

Wenn aus den Weltenweiten
Die Sonne spricht zum
Menschensinn
Und Freude aus den Seelentiefen
Dem Licht sich eint im Schauen,
Dann ziehen aus der Selbstheit
Hülle Gedanken in die
Raumesfernen
Und binden dumpf
Des Menschen Wesen an
Des Geistes Sein.

Verse 1 A
Easter Mood   *SPRING*

(Starts: on the 1st Sunday after 1st full Moon after the spring equinox.)

N: in late Mar. to late April
S: in late Sept. to late Oct.
(Dates: -   )

When from cosmic expanses
the sun speaks to human sense
and, in the beholding, joy
from depths of soul
unites to the light,
then from selfhood's sheath,
thoughts are upwards drawn
into the far distance,
and dimly bond human nature
to the spirit's being.

World-without: A & $\bar{\text{A}}$ (no.27)
World-within: 1 & 52

Verse 2 German

Ins Äussre des Sinnesalls
Verliert Gedankenmacht ihr
Eigensein;
Es finden Geisteswelten
Den Menschensprossen wieder,
Der seinen Keim in ihnen,
Doch seine Seelenfrucht
In sich muß finden.

(Note: verses 2 to 11 occur in the springtime and the early summertime, finishing on the day before the summer solstice verse, no.12. Their dates (& lengths of the weeks) vary, depending on how early or how late was the Eostre/Easter day.)

Verse 2 B

(Dates   -   )

In the senses' exterior world,[4]
thinking's power loses its
own being-ness;   *
The realms of spirit find again
the unfolding human offspring,   **
who must find its
seed-bud in them,
but its fruit of soul in itself.

(* '*being-ness*' means, its own nature,
   its own specific qualities)
(** '*offspring*', the German word
      implies 'a sprouting bud')

World-without: B & B̄   (no.28)
World-within: 2 & 51

---

[4] "*the senses' exterior...*": literally, 'in the
externality of the sensory world'

Verse 3   German

Es spricht zum Weltenall,
Sich selbst vergessend
Und seines Urstands eingedenk,
Des Menschen wachsend Ich:
In dir, befreiend mich
Aus meiner Eigenheiten Fessel,
Ergründe ich mein echtes Wesen.

Verse 3 C

(Dates: -   )

There speaks to the cosmos –
forgetful of itself, and mindful
of its primal state,
The growing 'I' of
the human being:
"In thee, freeing myself from
the shackles of my own
personality,
I fathom the depths
of my own being."

World-without: C & C̄   (no.29)
World-within: 3 & 50

Verse 4   German

Ich fühle Wesen meines Wesens,
So spricht Empfindung,
Die in der sonnerhellten Welt
Mit Lichtesfluten sich vereint;
Sie will dem Denken
Zur Klarheit Wärme schenken
Und Mensch und Welt
In Einheit fest verbinden.

Verse 4 D

(Dates: -   )

I feel the being-ness of my being –
thus speaks sentiency,
which, in the sun-illumined world
unites with cascades of light.
It wants to bestow warmth
on thinking's clarity,
and firmly bond into a unity
human beings and the world.

World-without: D & D̄   (no.30)
World-within: 4 & 49

Verse 5 German

Im Lichte, das aus Geistestiefen
Im Raume fruchtbar webend
Der Götter Schaffen offenbart.
In ihm erscheint der Seele Wesen
Geweitet zu dem Weltensein
Und auferstanden
Aus enger Selbstheit Innenmacht.

(The 3rd line in the manuscript has a full stop, and 3rd last line has *zum*, and not *zu dem,* but this longer version is needed for the iambic metre.)

Verse 5 E

(Dates: -   )

In the light that from spirit depths
fertilely weaves through space
the gods' creating manifests: *
in this appears the soul's nature
expanded out to cosmic being
and resurrected from
narrow selfhood's inner power.

(* "the gods": Biblical scholarship has
neglected this core spiritual concept,
which is fully accepted in many
religions and modes of spirituality. It
refers to divine-spiritual beings; these
deities are known in deeper mystical
Biblical traditions as the 'divine
hierarchies'.)

World-without: E & Ē   (no.31)
World-within: 5 & 48

Verse 6   German

Es ist erstanden aus der Eigenheit
Mein Selbst und findet sich
Als Weltenoffenbarung
In Zeit- und Raumeskräften;
Die Welt, sie zeigt mir überall
Als göttlich Urbild
Des eignen Abbilds Wahrheit.

Verse 6 F

(Dates   -   )

There has arisen, from its own
separateness my self,
and finds itself as
revelation of the cosmos,
in the powers of space and time.
Everywhere, the world
 – as divine archetype –
shows me the true nature
of my own reflected-image.[5]

World-without: F & $\overline{F}$ (no.32)
World-within: 6 & 47

---

[5] The earthly "I" is a reflected image of the
spiritual forces in creation.

Verse 7 German

Mein Selbst, es drohet zu
Entfliehen,
Vom Weltenlichte mächtig
Angezogen.
Nun trete du, mein Ahnen
In deine Rechte kräftig ein,
Ersetze mir des Denkens Macht,
Das in der Sinne Schein
Sich selbst verlieren will.

Verse 7 G

(Dates: -   )

My self, it's threatening to flee,
attracted powerfully
by cosmic light:
now enter, my divining, *
with strength,
into your rightful realm;
replace for me
my thinking's power which
in the senses' bright illusion
wants to lose itself.

(*"divining": is a poetic form of the
word, 'intuiting'.)

World-without: G & G̅   (no.33)
World-within: 7 & 46

Verse 8 German

Es wächst der Sinne Macht
Im Bunde mit der Götter Schaffen,
Sie drückt des Denkens Kraft
Zur Traumes Dumpfheit mir herab.
Wenn göttlich Wesen
Sich meiner Seele einen will,
Muss menschlich Denken
Im Traumessein sich still
bescheiden.

Verse 8 H

(Dates   -   )

The power of the senses grows
in union with the gods' creating,
it presses thinking's clarity down
to dreaming's dimness.
If the Divine would
unite to my soul,
human thinking must
humbly yield itself
to dream existence.

World-without: H & H̄   (no.34)
World-within: 8 & 45

Verse 9 German

Vergessend meine Willenseigenheit
Erfüllet Weltenwärme
sommerkündend
Mir Geist und Seelenwesen;
Im Licht mich zu verlieren
Gebietet mir das Geistesschauen,
Und kraftvoll kündet Ahnung mir:
Verliere dich, um dich zu finden.

Verse 9 I

(Dates: -   )

Forgetting my personal will,
cosmic warmth, heralding the
summer,
enfills my soul and spirit,
to lose myself in the light
– thus does spirit vision bid me –
and intuition, fore-sensing,
powerfully unto me proclaims:
"O lose yourself, to find yourself !"

World-without: I & I̱   (no.35)
World-within: 9 & 44

Verse 10 German

Zu sommerlichen Höhen
Erhebt der Sonne leuchtend
Wesen sich,
Es nimmt mein menschlich Fühlen
In seine Raumeswesen mit,
Erahnend regt im Innern sich
Empfindung, dumpf mir kündend,
Erkennen wirst du einst:
Dich fühlte jetzt ein Gotteswesen.

Verse 10 K

(Dates: -   )

Into summer heights
rises the sun's radiant being,
it takes my human feeling
into its wide expanse of space.
Intuiting, an inner sensing stirs
which faintly unto me proclaims,
"One day you will become aware:
a divine being has sensed you
now".

World-without: K & K̄ (no.36)
World-within: 10 & 43

Verse 11 German

Es ist in dieser Sonnenstunde
An dir, die weise Kunde zu
Erkennen,
An Weltenschönheit hingegeben,
In dir fühlend zu durchleben:
Verlieren kann das Menschen-Ich
Und finden sich im Welten-Ich.

(The German text is uncertain; possibly,
"In dir *dich* fuhlend zu durchleben")

Verse 11 L

(Dates: -   )

In this solar hour it is
incumbent upon you,
surrendered to the beauty
all around,
to discern the words of wisdom,
"Within you, feelingly experience:
The human I – it can lose itself
and find itself,
within the cosmic I."   [6]

world-without: L & L̄ (no.37)
world-within: 11 & 42

Note:
With verse 12, we come to the
hemisphere's summer solstice. In the
North this occurs between June 20th
and June 22nd; in the South, it occurs
between December 20th and 23rd. The
Christian world long ago, instituted
the Festival of *St. John's Tide* on the

---

[6] This verse has complex problems: see the
Appendix. Quotation marks are added by me for
clarity. See my *Annotated Soul Calendar* for
further details.

summer solstice day, to absorb old 'pagan' summer solstice festivities. The 'St. John' referred to is John the Baptist, who is traditionally viewed as being born on the summer solstice; but more importantly, in his aura, influences from solar deities were present. The 'cosmic I' refers to the high deities in the sun-sphere.

Its 'world-within' mirroring number is 41. This letter for this verse would normally be 'm'; but it actually has no letter assigned to it.

Johannes-Stimmung

Der Welten Schönheitsglanz,
Er zwinget mich aus Seelentiefen
Des Eigenlebens Götterkräfte
Zum Weltenfluge zu entbinden;
Mich selber zu verlassen,
Vertrauend nur mich suchend
In Weltenlicht und Weltenwärme.

Verse 12

St. John's Tide Mood

(N: 24th - 29th June
 S: 24th - 29th Dec.)

The world's radiant beauty, [7]
it compels me to release
from depths of soul for
cosmic flight
my own life's divine forces
– to leave myself –
trusting only to seek myself
in cosmic light and
cosmic warmth.

world-without: nil
world-within: 12 & 41

---

[7] "*The world's*" means, the local area of your
environs (your hemisphere).

Verse 13   German

Und bin ich in den Sinneshöhen,
So flammt in meinen Seelentiefen
Aus Geistes Feuerwelten
Der Götter Wahrheitswort:
In Geistesgründen suche ahnend
Dich geistverwandt zu finden.

Verse 13 M

(N: 30th June - 6th July
 S: 30th Dec. - 5th Jan.)

And when I am
in the senses' heights,
then there flames forth
in my soul's depths
from the fire-realms of the spirit,
the gods' word-of-truth: *
"In spirit depths seek intuitively
to find yourself as spirit-kindred".

(* '*gods*': see note to verse 5.)

world-without: M & M̄   (no.38)
world-within: 13 & 40

SOMMER

An Sinnesoffenbarung hingegeben
Verlor ich Eigenwesens Trieb,
Gedankentraum, er schien
Betäubend mir das Selbst
Zu rauben,
Doch weckend nahet schon
Im Sinnenschein mir
Weltendenken.

Verse 14 N

SUMMER

(N: 7th Jul - 13th July
 S: 6th Jan. - 12th Jan.)

To the senses' revelation
surrendered,
I lost my own being's
inherent drive.
Dream-thinking it seems,
benumbing,
to rob me of my self, and yet
already stirring,
there draws near to me
in the senses' shining semblance,
cosmic thinking.

World-without: N & N̄   (no.39)
World-within: 14 & 39

Verse 15 German

Ich fühle wie verzaubert
Im Weltenschein das Geistesweben,
Es hat in Sinnesdumpfheit
Gehüllt mein Eigenwesen,
Zu schenken mir die Kraft
Die, ohnmächtig sich selbst
Zu geben,
Mein Ich in seinen Schranken ist.

(See the Appendix for corrections
made to this verse.)

Verse 15 O
(N: 14th Jul - 20th July
 S: 13th Jan. - 19th Jan.)

I feel as if enchanted in
the world's bright semblance [8]
is the spirit's interweaving,
creative power.
It has enveloped my own being
in the senses' dimness,
to grant me the power
which my self, within
its narrow strictures,
is powerless to give unto itself.

World-without: O & Ō   (no.40)
World-within: 15 & 38

---

[8] '*the world's*' means, your local environs (i.e.,
hemisphere).

Verse 16 German

Zu bergen Geistgeschenk im
Innern,
Gebietet strenge mir mein Ahnen,
Dass reifend Gottesgaben
In Seelengründen fruchtend
Der Selbstheit Früchte bringen.

Verse 16 P

(N: 21st Jul - 27th July
 S: 20th Jan. - 26th Jan.)

To shelter spirit gift
within my inner being,
my intuition sternly bids me,
so that ripening gifts of God –
fructifying in the soul's depths,
may bring fruits to the selfhood.

World-without: P & P̄   (no.41)
World-within: 16 & 37

Sommer

Es spricht das Weltenwort,
Das ich durch Sinnestore
In Seelengründe durfte führen:
Erfülle deine Geistestiefen
Mit meinen Weltenweiten,
Zu finden einstens mich in dir.

Verse 17   Q

Summer

(N: 28th Jul - 3rd Aug.
 S: 27th Jan. - 2nd Feb.)

The cosmic Word speaks,
which I may guide
through senses' portals
into the soul's foundations:
"Enfill your spirit's depths
with my cosmic expanses,
to find, one future day,
Me in you".

(This second heading "Summer" is
from Rudolf Steiner.)

World-without: Q & Q̄   (no.42)
World-within: 17 & 36

Verse 18 German

Kann ich die Seele weiten,
Dass sie sich selbst verbindet
Empfangnem Welten-Keimesworte?
Ich ahne, daß ich Kraft muß finden,
Die Seele würdig zu gestalten
Zum Geistes-Kleide sich zu bilden.

Verse 18 R

(N: 4th Aug. - 10th Aug.
 S: 3rd Feb. - 9th Feb.)

Can I expand the soul,
that it unites itself
to the germinal cosmic Word?
I intuit that I must find the power
to worthily form the soul,
to mould it into
a vestment of the spirit.

World-without: R & R̄ (no.43)
World-within: 18 & 35

Verse 19   German

Geheimnisvoll das Neu-Empfang'ne
Mit der Erinnerung zu
Umschließen,
Sei meines Strebens weitrer Sinn,
Es soll erstarkend Eigenkräfte
In meinem Innern wecken
Und werdend mich mir selber
Geben.

(See the Appendix for corrections
made to this verse.)

Verse 19   S
(N: 11th Aug. - 17th Aug.
 S: 10th Feb. - 16th Feb.)

To enclose mysteriously
the Newly-Received [9]
with the memory –
may this be
the further purpose
of my striving,
which shall awaken
my own strengthened forces
in my inner being
and evolving on,
give my Self to me.

World-without: S & S̄   (no.44)
World-within: 19 & 34

---

[9] This is a spiritual influence from cosmic forces
present in the summer heights (which assists
the Atman or Spirit-human to develop).

Verse 20 German

So fühl ich erst mein Sein;   *
Das fern vom Welten-Dasein
In sich, sich selbst erlöschen
Und bauend nur auf eignem
Grunde
An sich, sich selbst ertöten müsste.

(See the Appendix for corrections
made to this verse.)

(* The semi-colon here is in the
manuscript.)

Verse 20 T
(N: 18th Aug. - 24th Aug.
 S: 17th Feb. - 23rd Feb.)

Only now do I feel my being;
which far from cosmic existence
within itself, would
extinguish itself,
and building solely upon
its own foundation, would,
for itself, only deaden itself.

World-without: T & T̄ (no.45)
World-within: 20 & 33

Verse 21 German

Ich fühle fruchtend fremde Macht
Sich stärkend mir mich selbst
Verleihen,
Den Keim empfind ich reifend
Und Ahnung lichtvoll weben
In Innern an der Selbstheit Macht.

Verse 21   U
(N: 25th Aug. - 31st Aug.
 S: 24th Feb. - 1st Mar.)

I feel an unknown force ripening,
growing stronger
it grants my Self to me;
The seed bud I sense maturing,
and intuition weaving
brightly within me
for my selfhood's power.

World-without: U & U̅   (no.46)
World-within: 21 & 32

Verse 22   German

Das Licht aus Weltenweiten
Im Innern lebt es kräftig fort,
Es wird zum Seelenlichte
Und leuchtet in die Geistestiefen,
Um Früchte zu entbinden,
Die Menschenselbst aus
Weltenselbst
Im Zeitenlaufe reifen lassen.

Verse 22 V

(N: 1st Sept. - 7th Sept.
S: 2nd Mar. - 8th Mar.)

The light from cosmic expanses –
it lives on powerfully within me,
it becomes soul light
and shines in spirit depths
that fruits may be released
which allow in the course of time
the human self to ripen out of
the cosmic self.

World-without: V & V̄   (no.47)
World-within: 22 & 31

Verse 23   German

Es dämpfet herbstlich sich
Der Sinne Reizesstreben;
In Lichtesoffenbarung mischen
Der Nebel dumpfe Schleier sich.
Ich selber schau in Raumesweiten
Des Herbstes Weltenschlaf.
Der Sommer hat an mich
Sich selber hingegeben.

(See the Appendix for corrections to
this verse.)

Verse 23 W

(N: 8th Sept. - 14th Sept.
 S: 9th Mar. - 15th Mar.)

The senses' striving for stimulation
autumnally dampens down;
in the light's manifestation
is mingled now the fog's dim veil.
I myself now behold autumn's
sleep, all around me
and far into the distance.
The summer has given
itself unto me.

World-without: W & W̄   (no.48)
World-within: 23 & 30

Verse 24   German

Sich selbst erschaffen stets,
Wird Seelensein sich selbst gewahr;
Der Weltengeist, er strebet fort
In Selbsterkenntnis neu belebt
Und schafft aus Seelenfinsternis
Des Selbstsinns Willensfrucht.

Verse 24 X
(N: 15th Sept. - 21st Sept.
S: 16th Mar. - 22nd Mar.)

Continually creating itself,
soul-being becomes self-aware;
The World-Spirit, it onward strives,
through self-cognition
enlivened anew,
and creates out of soul darkness
the fruits of will
of the sense of self.*

World-without: X & X̄   (no.49)
World-within: 24 & 29

* This unusual phrase, '*fruits of will*'
maintains a parallel to the fruiting
processes happening in Nature.

Verse 25 German

Ich darf nun mir gehören
Und leuchtend breiten Innenlicht
In Raumes- und in Zeitenfinsternis.
Zum Schlafe drängt natürlich
Wesen,
Der Seele Tiefen sollen wachen
Und wachend tragen Sonnengluten -
Du kaltes Winterfluten.

(See the Appendix for corrections
made to this verse.)

Verse 25 Y

(starts as from the autumn equinox
day)
(N: 22nd Sept. - 28th Sept.
S: 24th Mar. - 30th Mar.)

I now may belong unto myself
and luminous, spread inner light
into the darkness
of space and time.
The natural world
is drawn into sleep.
The soul's depths shall awaken
and waking, maintain
a fiery solar glow – [10]
Thou cold surging-flow of winter. *

(* At the autumn equinox, the soul
defiantly resolves not to be inwardly
subdued by the outer and inner
coldness of winter, when it comes.)

World-without: Y & $\bar{\text{Y}}$ (no. 50)
World-within: 25 & 28

---

[10] I have added this dash to make the dramatic
personification clearer.

Verse 26 German

Michaeli-Stimmung

Natur, dein mütterliches Sein,
Ich trage es in meinem
Willenswesen;
Und meines Willens Feuermacht,
Sie stählet meines Geistestriebe,
Dass die gebären Selbstgefühl
Zu tragen mich in mir.

Verse 26   Z

The Mood of Michaelmas

(N: 29th Sept. - 5th Oct.
 S: 29th Mar. - 4th April)

Nature – thy maternal being,
I bear this within my will;
and the fire-force of my will
steels the impulses of my spirit,
to beget self-awareness,
that my Self may be borne along
within me.

World-without: Z & Z̄   (no.52)
World-within: 26 & 27

Verse 27 German

In meines Wesens Tiefen dringen:
Erregt ein ahnungsvolles Sehnen
Dass ich mich selbstetrachtend
finde
Als Sommersonnengabe,
Die als Keim
In Herbstesstimmung
Wärmend lebt
Als meiner Seele Kräftetrieb.

Verse 27 $\overline{\text{A}}$
(N: 6th Oct. - 12th Oct.
S: 5th April - 11th April)

To penetrate into my being's
depths –
a yearning is stirring,
foresensing, that now,
in self-observation
I may find myself as gift
of the summer sun, which
as a seed, warmingly lives
in the mood of autumn,
as my soul's driving force.

World-without: $\overline{\text{A}}$ & A   (no. 1)
World-within: 27 & 26

Verse 28 German

Ich kann im Innern neu belebt
Erfüllen eignen Wesens Weiten
Und krafterfüllt Gedankenstrahlen
Aus Seelensonnenmacht
Den Lebensrätseln lösend spenden,
Erfüllung manchem
Wunsche leihen
Dem Hoffnung schon
Die Schwingen lähmte.

(See the Appendix for corrections
made to this verse.)

Verse 28 B̄

(N: 13th Oct. - 19th Oct.
 S: 12th April - 18th April)

Renewed in my inner being,
I can encompass the breadth
of my own nature, and from
the sun-strength of the soul
send forth empowered
rays of thought,
resolving riddles of life,
granting fulfilment to
many a wish whose wings
mere hoping has already lamed.

World-without: B̄ & B (no. 2)
World-within: 28 & 25

Verse 29 German

Sich selbst des Denkens Leuchten
Im Innern kraftvoll zu entfachen,
Erlebtes sinnvoll deutend
Aus Weltengeistes Kräftequell,
Ist mir nun Sommererbe,
Ist Herbstesruhe
Und auch Winterhoffnung.

Verse 29   C̄

(N: 20th Oct. - 26th Oct.
 S: 19th April - 25th April)

To enkindle by oneself,
powerfully within,
the radiance of thinking
from the Cosmos-Spirit's
fountain of strength,
disclosing the meaning of
life's experiences,
is now for me,
summer's heritage,
is autumn's peace
and also winter's hope.

World-without: C̄ & C (no. 3)
World-within: 29 & 24

Verse 30 German

Es sprießen mir im
Seelensonnenlicht
Des Denkens reife Früchte,
In Selbstbewußtseins Sicherheit
Verwandelt alles Fühlen sich.
Empfinden kann ich freudevoll
Des Herbstes Geisterwachen,
Der Winter wird in mir
Den Seelensommer wecken.

Verse 30 D̄

(N: 27th Oct. - 2nd Nov.
 S: 26th April - 2nd May)

To me, are sprouting now
in the soul's sunlight *
the ripened fruits of thinking.
In the assuredness of
self-awareness
all feeling transforms.
Joyously, I can sense
the autumn's spirit-awakening.
The winter shall awaken in me
the summer of the soul.

(* 'To me...': that is, this deeper
thinking is what I'm now experiencing)

World-without: D̄ & D   (no. 4)
World-within: 30 & 23

Verse 31 German

Das Licht aus Geistestiefen,
Nach außen strebt es sonnenhaft,
Es wird zur Lebenswillenskraft
Und leuchtet in der
Sinne Dumpfheit,
Um Kräfte zu entbinden,
Die Schaffensmächte aus
Seelentrieben
Im Menschenwerke reifen lassen.

Verse 31 E̅

(N: 3rd Nov. - 9th Nov.
S: 3rd May - 9th May)

The light from spiritual depths –
like sunlight, it strives to ray forth,
becoming life's power of will,
and shines in the dullness
of the senses,
to release forces which let ripen
from the soul's impulses,
creative powers
within human deeds.

World-without: E̅ & E (no. 5)
World-within: 31 & 22

Verse 32   German

Ich fühle fruchtend eigene Kraft
Sich stärkend mich der
Welt verleihn;
Mein Eigenwesen fühl ich kraftend
Zur Klarheit sich zu wenden
Im Lebensschicksalsweben.

Verse 32 F̄
(N: 10th Nov. - 16th Nov.
 S: 10th May - 16th May)

I feel my own power
bearing fruit;
growing in strength,
it gives me to the world.
My own being I feel
strengthening, seeking clarity
in weaving the tapestry
of life's destiny.

World-without: F̄ & F (no. 6)
World-within: 32 & 21

Verse 33   German

So fühl ich erst die Welt,
Die ausser meiner Seele Miterleben
An sich nur frostig leeres Leben
Und ohne Macht sich offenbarend,
In Seelen sich von neuem
Schaffend,
In sich den Tod nur finden könnte.

(The Appendix notes a textual
 difficulty with this verse.)

Verse 33 $\overline{G}$
(N: 17th Nov. - 23rd Nov.
 S: 17th May - 23rd May)

Only now do I feel the world, [11]
which, deprived of my soul's
experiencing,
is disempowered in itself,
manifesting only frosty, empty life;
creating itself anew in souls –
in itself, would find only death.

World-without: $\overline{G}$ & G (no. 7)
World-within: 33 & 20

---

[11] *'the world'* means, the local area of your
environs (hemisphere).

Verse 34 German

Geheimnisvoll das Alt-Bewahrte
Mit neu erstandem Eigensein
Im Innern sich belebend fühlen:
Es soll erweckend Weltenkräfte
In meines Lebens
Außenwerk ergießen
Und werdend mich ins
Dasein prägen.

Verse 34 H̄

(N: 24th Nov. - 30th Nov.
 S: 24th May - 30th May)

To sense the Treasure
preserved from long ago,   *
newly arisen with its own
being-ness,
mysteriously quickening
itself within me:
it shall pour awakened
cosmic forces
into my life's external deeds
and, evolving on, imprint me
into existence.

* (from the summer's in-breath, as in
    verse 19, and retained.)

World-without: H̄ & H   (no. 8)
World-within: 34 & 19

Verse 35 German

Kann ich das Sein erkennen
Dass es sich wiederfindet
Im Seelenschaffensdrange?
Ich fühle, dass mir Macht verleih'n
Das eigne Selbst dem Weltenselbst
Als Glied bescheiden einzuleben.

Verse 35 $\overline{\text{I}}$
(N: 1st Dec. - 7th Dec.
 S: 31st May - 6th June)

Can I so recognize existence
that it finds itself again
in the soul's creative impulses?
I feel that power is granted me,
to merge my own self humbly
into the Self of the Cosmos.

World-without: $\overline{\text{I}}$ & I (no. 9)
World-within: 35 & 18

Verse 36 German

In meines Wesens Tiefen spricht
Zur Offenbarung drängend
Geheimnisvoll das Weltenwort:
Erfülle deiner Arbeit Ziele
Mit meinem Geisteslichte,
Zu opfern dich durch mich.

Verse 36 $\overline{\text{K}}$
(N: 8th Dec. - 14th Dec.
 S: 7th June - 13th June)

In the depths of my being
speaks mysteriously
the cosmic Word
– impelled to revelation –
"Let the goals of your work
with my spirit light be filled,
to offer up yourself through me".

World-without: $\overline{\text{K}}$ & K (no. 10)
World-within: 36 & 17

Verse 37 German

Zu tragen Geisteslicht in
Weltenwinternacht
Erstrebet selig meines
Herzens Trieb,
Dass leuchtend Seelenkeime
In Weltengründen wurzeln,
Und Gotteswort im Sinnesdunkel
Verklärend alles Sein durchtönt.

Verse 37 $\overline{L}$
(N: 15th Dec. - 21st Dec.
 S: 14th June - 20th June)

To bear the spirit's light within the
earth's winter night,   *
aspires blissfully my heart's desire,
that soul seeds, glowing bright,
take root in cosmic depths,
and the Word of God
in senses' darkness resounds,
enkindling light within all being.

(This verse ends on the winter solstice
day and heralds the Holy Nights of
your hemisphere's wintertime.)

(*The hemisphere's winter 'night')

World-without: $\overline{L}$ & L (no. 11)
World-within: 37 & 16

Comment: When it is the winter-solstice Yuletide in one hemisphere, it is the Summer Solstice in the other hemisphere.

"Just consider, though, that when we here [*in Europe*] have the St. John's Tide festival (*in the summertime*), that is, when it is the case that our souls can follow the Earth-soul which arises and unites itself with the stars, then the Antipodes, the Antipodeans, have their Holy Nights (*Yuletide*)."

Whilst [*during summer*] in the north[*ern hemisphere*] the Earth-soul goes forth, appearing to spiritual vision like a comet's tail which is drawing itself out toward heaven, on the other side [*of the Earth*] the Earth-soul withdraws back into the earth and it is Christmas-Holy Nights (*festival time*} there {*in that hemisphere*}."

(Rudolf Steiner, May 21, 1923, GA 226)

Verse 38 German

Weihe-Nacht-Stimmung

Ich fühle wie entzaubert
Das Geisteskind im Seelenschoß;
Es hat in Herzenshelligkeit
Gezeugt das heil'ge Weltenwort
Der Hoffnung Himmelsfrucht,
Die jubelnd wächst in
Weltenfernen
Aus meines Wesens Gottesgrund.

Verse 38 M̄

Holy Nights Mood

(N: 22nd Dec. - 28th Dec.
 S: 21st June - 27th June)

I feel as from enchantment freed
the Spirit Child in my soul's womb:
in radiance of the heart
the holy cosmic Word
has now begotten
the heavens' fruit of hope
which jubilantly grows in
distant realms
from my own being's
divine foundations.

World-without: M̄ & M   (No.13)
World-within: 38 & 15

Verse 39 German

An Geistesoffenbarung hingegeben
Gewinne ich des Weltenwesens
Licht.
Gedankenkraft, sie wächst
Sich klärend mir mich selbst
Zu geben,
Und weckend löst sich mir
Aus Denkermacht das
Selbstgefühl.

Verse 39 N̄

(N: 29th Dec. - 4th Jan.
 S: 28th June - 4th July)

Devoted to revelations of the
spirit,
I attain the light of cosmic being.
The power of thinking, it grows,
clarifying, it gives my Self to me;
and self-awareness, awakening,
emerges for me, from Thinker's
power.

World-without: N̄ & N (no. 14)
World-within: 39 & 14

Verse 40 German

Und bin ich in den Geistestiefen,
Erfüllt in meinen Seelengründen
Aus Herzens Liebewelten
Der Eigenheiten leerer Wahn
Sich mit des
Weltenwortes Feuerkraft.

Verse 40 $\overline{\text{O}}$
(N: 5th Jan. - 11th Jan.
 S: 5th July - 11th July)

And, if I am in the spirit's depths,
then in my soul's foundations
the empty delusion
of my own self is filled   *
 – from the heart's worlds of love –
with the fiery might
of the cosmic Word.

(* Here '*self*' refers to the normal
personality.)

World-without: $\overline{\text{O}}$ & O   (no. 15)
World-within: 40 & 13

Verse 41 German

Der Seele Schaffensmacht,
Sie strebet aus dem
Herzensgrunde,
Im Menschenleben Götterkräfte
Zu rechtem Wirken zu entflammen,
Sich selber zu gestalten
In Menschenliebe und im
Menschenwerke.

Verse 41 $\overline{P}$
(N: 12th Jan. -18th Jan.
S: 12th July - 18th July)

The soul's creative might:
it is striving from the heart's
foundations
to rightly enkindle forces of the
gods in human activity,
to mould itself in human love
and in human deeds.

World-without: $\overline{P}$ & P (no. 16)
World-within: 41 & 12

Verse 42 German

Es ist in diesem Winterdunkel
Die Offenbarung eigner Kraft
Der Seele starker Trieb,
In Finsternisse sie zu lenken
Und ahnend vorzufühlen
Durch Herzenswärme
Sinnesoffenbarung.

Verse 42   Q̄

(N: 19th Jan. - 25th Jan.
 S: 19th July - 25th July)

In this wintry gloom
it is the soul's strong impulse
to manifest its own power,
to guide itself in the darknesses;
and to intuitively feel in advance
through warmth of heart,
the senses' revelations.

World-without: Q̄ & Q   (no. 17)
World-within: 42 & 11

Verse 43 German

In winterlichen Tiefen
Erwarmt des Geistes wahres Sein;
Es gibt dem Weltenscheine
Durch Herzenskräfte
Daseinsmächte;
Der Weltenkälte trotzt erstarkend
Das Seelenfeuer im
Menscheninnern.

Verse 43   R̄

(N: 26th Jan. - 1st Feb.
S: 26th July - 1st Aug.)

In wintry depths grows warm
true being of the spirit;
it gives to world-semblance, *
through forces of the heart,
an empowered existence.
Defying the world's coldness   **
the soul-fire
within the human being
grows stronger.

(* '*world-semblance*': the material
world as Maya, as illusory, in so far as
it gives the impression that it is
complete unto itself, that only matter
exists.)

(** *The world's*: the local area of your
hemisphere.)

World-without: R̄ & R   (no. 18)
World-within: 43 & 10

Verse 44 German

Ergreifend neue Sinnesreize
Erfüllet Seelenklarheit,
Eingedenk vollzogner Geistgeburt,
Verwirrend sprossend
Weltenwerden
Mit meines Denkens
Schöpferwillen.

Verse 44 $\overline{S}$

(N: 2nd Feb. - 8th Feb.
 S: 2nd Aug. - 8th Aug.)

Clarity of soul, grasping new
sensory stimuli, and mindful
of accomplished spirit-birth,
enfills the world's bewildering, *
sprouting, surging growing
with my thinking's creative will.

(* *the world's*: means, the local area
of your environs, that is, hemisphere).

World-without: $\overline{S}$ & S (no. 19)
World-within: 44 & 9

Verse 45 German

Es festigt sich Gedankenmacht
Im Bunde mit der Geistgeburt,
Sie hellt der Sinne dumpfe Reize
Zur vollen Klarheit auf.
Wenn Seelenfülle sich
mit dem Weltenwerden einen will,
Muss Sinnesoffenbarung
Des Denkens Licht empfangen.

Verse 45   T̄

N: 9th Feb. - 15th Feb.
 S: 9th Aug. - 15th Aug.)

Power of thought grows firm
in union with the spirit-birth,
which brightens the senses' dull
inciting into full clarity. *
If fullness of soul
wants to unite with
the world's ongoing evolving **
then what the senses reveal
must receive the light of thinking.

(* *'brightens the senses dull...'* that is,
empowered, intuitive consciousness
can 'find the concept belonging to the
percept': that is, perceive the Idea
behind the sensory object.)

** *the world's*: the local area of your
hemisphere.)

World-without: T̄ & T (no. 20)
World-within: 45 & 8

Verse 46 German

Die Welt, sie drohet zu betäuben
Der Seele eingebor'ne Kraft;
Nun trete du, Erinnerung,
Aus Geistestiefen leuchtend auf
Und stärke mir das Schauen,
Das nur durch Willenskräfte
Sich selbst erhalten kann.

Verse 46 $\overline{\text{U}}$

(N: 16th Feb. - 22nd Feb.
S: 16th Aug. - 22nd Aug.)

The world – it threatens *
to benumb the force
born within the soul.
Now come forth, remembrance,
from spiritual depths, radiantly,
and strengthen spiritual seeing
for me, which can maintain itself
only through powers of the will.

(* 'world': the local area of your environs
(hemisphere).

World-without: $\overline{\text{U}}$ & U (no. 21)
World-within: 46 & 7

Verse 47 German

Es will erstehen aus dem
Weltenschoße,
Den Sinneschein erquickend,
Werdelust.
Sie finde meines Denkens Kraft
Gerüstet durch die Götterkräfte,
Die kräftig mir in Innern leben.

Verse 47 $\overline{V}$
(N: 23rd Feb. - 29th Feb.
S: 23rd Aug. - 29th Aug.)

There wants to arise from the
world's womb [12]
enjoyment of Becoming,
quickening the senses' radiance.
May it find my thinking's power
armoured through the powers
of the gods,
which powerfully live within me.

'Becoming' (Werden): translates a
core German concept: 'on-going
evolving', and means here: 'fertile
growth which is bringing forth new
life'.

(One word here was uncertain, see the
Appendix.)

World-without: $\overline{V}$ & V (no. 22)
World-within: 47 & 6

---

[12] 'the world's womb': means, the hemisphere's
etheric and astral energies.

Verse 48 German

Im Lichte, das aus Weltenhöhen
Der Seele machtvoll fließen will,
Erscheine, lösend Seelenrätsel,
Des Weltendenkens Sicherheit,
Versammelnd seiner
Strahlen Macht,
Im Menschenherzen
Liebe weckend.

Verse 48   W̄

(N: 1st Mar. - 7th Mar.
 S: 30th Aug. - 5th Sept.)

In the light which
from cosmic heights
wants to flow powerfully
into the soul,
may there appear,
resolving life's riddles,
the sureness of cosmic thinking
gathering the power of its rays,
awakening love in
the human heart.

World-without: W̄ & W   (no. 23)
World-within: 48 & 5

Verse 49 German

Ich fühle Kraft des Weltenseins:
So spricht Gedankenklarheit,
Gedenkend eignen
Geistes Wachsen
In finstern Weltennächten,
Und neigt dem nahen Weltentage
Des innern Hoffnungsstrahlen.

Verse 49 $\overline{\text{X}}$
(N: 8th Mar. - 14th Mar.
S: 6th Sept. - 12th Sept.)

"I sense the power of the world's
being" [13]
so speaks clarity of thought,
recalling its own spiritual growth
in the gloom of the world's nights,
and to the approaching world-day
it now inclines the rays of inner
hope.

('*the world's nights*': winter, in the local area of
your hemisphere.)

('*world-day*': the spring equinox day & the
days/weeks thereafter.)

World-without: $\overline{\text{X}}$ & X (no. 24)
World-within: 49 & 4

---

[13] *the world's*: your hemisphere and cosmic
influences active in it.

Verse 50 German

Es spricht zum Menschen-Ich,
Sich machtvoll offenbarend,
Und seines Wesens Kräfte lösend
Des Weltendaseins Werdelust:
In dich mein Leben tragend
Aus seinem Zauberbanne,
Erreiche ich mein wahres Ziel.

(Note: this verse ends on the day before the spring equinox, which can occur between Mar. 19-21st in the north, and between Sept. 22-23rd in the south.)

Verse 50 $\overline{Y}$
(N: 15th Mar. - 21st Mar.
 S: 13th Sept. - 22nd Sept.)

There speaks to the human "I",
powerfully manifesting itself and
releasing forces of its being, the
world's enjoyment in Becoming.
"Bearing my life in thee,
out of its enchantment,
I may attain my true goal."

('*the world's enjoyment...*' means: the
eagerness of the various beings in the
hemisphere to encourage fertile
growth.)

('*Becoming*': see note for v. 47.)

World-without: $\overline{Y}$ & Y (no. 25)
World-within: 50 & 3

Verse 51 German

Frühlung-Erwartung

Ins Innre des Menschenwesens
Ergiesst der Sinne Reichtum sich,
Es findet sich der Weltengeist
Im Spiegelbild des Menschenauges,
Das seine Kraft aus ihm
Sich neu erschaffen muß.

Verse 51

Awaiting Spring

Note: this verse starts on the spring
equinox day.

(Dates: -   )
*The week for this verse, and the next
verse, often need to be made shorter
or longer.*

Into the human being
the senses pour their
rich abundance.
The Cosmos-Spirit finds itself
in the mirror-image
of the human eye;
which from this Spirit
has to create its strength anew.

World-without: ~
World-within: 51 & 2

(As with verse 38, verse 51 has no
letter given to it.)

Verse 52 German

Wenn aus den Seelentiefen
Der Geist sich wendet zu dem
Weltensein
Und Schönheit quillt aus
Raumesweiten,
Dann ziehet aus Himmelsfernen
Des Lebens Kraft in
Menschenleiber
Und einet, machtvoll wirkend,
Des Geistes Wesen mit dem
Menschensein.

(Line 3: *ziehet* is used here: the
poetic archaic form of *zieht*.)

Verse 52 $\overline{Z}$

(Dates: -   )
(Ends on the Saturday prior to the 1st
Sunday after the 1st Full Moon, after
your hemisphere's spring equinox
day.)

When, from the depths of the soul,
the spirit turns toward
the external world,
and beauty wells forth
from far and wide,
then from distant heavens,
the Life-force draws into
human bodies,
and, powerfully active,
unites the spirit's being
with human existence.

World-without: $\overline{Z}$ & Z   (no. 26)
World-within: 52 & 1

APPENDIX 1: Verses corrected because of unauthorized changes

Verse 11, lines 2 & 4

The official text, based on the 1912 edition with its unauthorized changes, has a colon at the end of line 2, which has put emphasis upon the state of being "surrendered to the beauty all around". But the only emphasis in this verse created by a colon, is that made by Rudolf Steiner, when he placed the only colon for this verse at the end of the third last line:

> "Within you, feelingly
> experience:
> The human I – it can lose itself
> and find itself, within the
> cosmic I.

Also, the word 'self' (*dich*) in line 4 is probably not there; the manuscript has only a very faint scribble. If it were there, it would mean:

> *"In you, feeling your Self,*
> *experience (this):*

But amongst other concerns, it appears to me unlikely that our soul, if it achieves an awareness of a 'higher' Self within, could lose awareness of this 'self', and then re-find it on a yet higher level, as a cosmic "I". Moreover, the presence of the word 'yourself' in this line seems to contradict the core message of the verse, which otherwise is about how, within a feeling-based experience of one's normal personality or self, the soul should strive to realize that one's earthly sense of self can be lost, and then found again – but found again as a higher, cosmic "I", up in the cosmic-solar influences active in the summer. This process seems to exclude any empowered self existing already in the personality, and making this discovery.

But see my *Annotated Soul's Calendar* for a more extensive commentary on what may possibly be an extra word in this line.

Verse 15 line 2:

The meaning of this verse has suffered severely through the changes made in 1912.

The words, **das Geistesweben** were changed in 1912 to:

> **des Geistes Weben**.

The first half of the verse is then incorrect, because the two alterations present this meaning:

> I feel as if (*I am*) enchanted in the
> radiant world's spirit Weaving (*i.e., tapestry*).
> > It (*the radiant world's semblance*) has enveloped my own being.....

But what Rudolf Steiner originally wrote, meant;

> I feel as if enchanted
> in the world's bright semblance
> is the spirit's interweaving
> creative power.
> This* has enveloped in sensory dimness my own being.......

(* *spirit's interweaving creative power*)

In other words, the reader, in contemplating nature, feels that now, in this warm summertime, the spirit's interweaving, creative activity **itself** is enchanted within the illusory material world, which in the summer is so bright, so empowered.

Secondly, another very important part of the meaning – which the changes of 1912 have deleted – is this: the human being has been enveloped in this semblance, **by of the spirit's active, living, interweaving creative power, for a specific purpose**.

Verse 19, Line 4:

In 1912, the word "Es" was changed to "Er":

Er soll erstarkend Eigenkräfte

This change moves the thing doing the action, from the 'striving', to the 'purpose'. This meant that it was no longer **the striving** which has the goal of "awakening strengthened forces...", but the "further purpose" has this goal.

The original wording from Rudolf Steiner declares that it is the striving which sets out to achieve something, and it does this by awakening renewed soul forces. This goal is "the further purpose"; and this purpose is achieved by one's striving.

Verse 20, last line:

In the official version, in 1912, the word 'an', was removed and replaced by "in" in the last line:

In sich sich selbst ertöten müßte.
(within itself, would deaden itself)

But Rudolf Steiner had written:
An sich, sich selbst ertöten müßte.

This original, correct text means:
"for itself, deaden itself."

That is, 'with regard to itself' deaden itself.

This is a much less drastic statement: the person is not about to undertake a 'killing-off' process inside itself. In reality, it is indicating that a subtle benumbing of consciousness may occur.

Verse 23, line 6:

In line 6 of the official version is the incorrect text:

>   Des Herbstes **Winter**schlaf.
>   (autumn's winter-sleep)

Rudolf Steiner actually wrote:
>   Des Herbstes **Welten**schlaf.

This original text literally means:
>   "autumn's world-sleep."

The 1912 change results in a mixing-up of autumn and winter; an intrusion of one season into the other. The original meaning is about the autumn environs around one.

But since 'world-sleep' can give the wrong impression, of a global sleep, whereas a hemispherical autumnal condition is meant, I have chosen an alternative, somewhat longer phrase, about one's local 'world': 'all around me, and far into the distance.'

Verse 25, last line:

In the official edition there is an error in the last line, taken up from the 1912 edition: the word "in". For Rudolf Steiner had in fact written,

> Du kalte*(s)* Winterfluten.

Not: **In** kalte Winterfluten.

For the publisher in 1912 to remove the word 'Du' (*thou*) and replace it with 'In' (*in*), was a serious error. One reason for this change being made is that the line, as it stands in the manuscript, does not have any clear meaning. But by inserting 'in', this line does make sense:

> In kalte (*plural*) Winterfluten
> =   in cold winter floods

In other words, because the phrase "Du kalte Winterfluten" is not a correct phrase, (there is a very minor error in the spelling of one word), the publisher decided this line was about winter floods, (which it is not), and changed the line in a major way. Floods are not a key feature of the winter in The Soul's Calendar; the inner astral-etheric qualities are. Also, very importantly, the word "Du" is clearly, specifically written; it cannot simply be deleted.

Since Rudolf Steiner used the singular word 'Thou' (Du), this means that 'Winterfluten' is also a singular word; yet this word is almost always a plural word. So one reason for the confusion and hence the altered official version, is that the word "Winterfluten', if viewed as a singular noun, is a very rare word; even academics can be unaware of it. So the editors decided to view it as a plural word.

But the correct solution here is, to conclude that Rudolf Steiner accidentally left an 's' off 'kalte'. So he meant to write, (as I have indicated above, in small fonts, within brackets):

Du kaltes Winterfluten.

This corrected text now means, in English:

Thou cold, surging-flow of winter.

So, the soul is looking ahead to when winter arrives, and triumphantly declares, directly to winter itself (which is here personified), that the soul shall maintain an inner soul-warmth, regardless of the cold surging-flow, physical and astral, underlying the winter time.

This word, in a rare singular usage as, 'surging-flow', is used by Rudolf Steiner several other times in his lectures.

There is another word in the manuscript with exactly the same error, namely, a missing 's'; it is verse 27, line 3. This was no doubt caused by the manuscript being written in haste, due to many other demands he was facing. This line in verse 25 is so awkward for editors, that it is not mentioned at all in the official editorial notes by the Archives about The Soul's Calendar.

Verse 28, line 2:

In the official version, line 2, is the changed text:
   Erfühlen eignen Wesens Weiten

I can dimly sense within, the extent of my own being,

But Rudolf Steiner wrote:
   Erfüllen eignen Wesens Weiten

This correct original text literally means:
   I can enfill my own being's expanses

This is more naturally expressed in English as,

   I can encompass the breadth of my own being

This original wording only is consistent with the message of the verse: namely, that the soul is now strongly empowered, and hence really able to achieve its goals. The weaker, changed version is fully inconsistent with the main theme of self-empowerment in the verse: "granting fulfilment to many a wish..." If one can only faintly sense one's own self, then the soul can't "grant fulfilment to many a wish".

Verse 33 German

So fühl ich erst die Welt,
Die außer meiner Seele Miterleben
An sich nur frostig leeres Leben
Und ohne Macht sich offenbarend,
In Seelen sich von neuem schaffend,
In sich den Tod nur finden könnte.

The last two lines in the published version when translated are:
  "creating itself anew in souls –
  in itself, would find only death."

But Rudolf Steiner wrote in line 5,

„In Seelen sich vom neuen schaffend",

this could mean, "in souls, creating itself from the new". But it is an awkward phrase, not fully grammatically correct, and of unclear meaning. So the reversal of the last letters in the two words was probably an error. The official edition has corrected this accidental reversal.

Verse 47: An unclear word

*There wants to arise from the world's
womb
enjoyment of Becoming,
quickening the senses' radiance.
May it find my thinking's power
armoured through the
powers of the gods,
which powerfully live within me.*

Line 5 in my translation has the
expression "the powers of the gods".
The original German text has
"Gotterkräfte", which is not a word: It
appears that Rudolf Steiner wrote 'o'
accidentally, instead of ö.

It is officially interpreted as
"Gotteskräfte", which does not need
an ö, and means "powers of God". But
careful examination of the original
manuscript shows that it is not an 's'
but an 'r' in this word. So meant is
"Götterkräfte" ("powers of the gods").

For Rudolf Steiner wrote an 's', (if
occurring in the middle of a word),
quite differently to the centre letter in
this word; also after every such 's', he
has always left a slight gap. There is
no gap here. So the letter is an 'r',
written here exactly as it is in all other
words in the manuscript.

Appendix 2: Glossary of some key terms

Cosmos-Spirit (Weltengeist) vs. 29, 51: a core spiritual being of the sun-sphere, together with associated beings and their influences.

cosmic thinking (Weltendenken) v. 14: the cosmic consciousness of the gods.

cosmic Word (Weltenwort): vs. 17,18,36, 40: influences raying forth from high cosmic beings; it is implied here that planetary and zodiac energies are involved.

Word of God (Gotteswort) v. 38: of similar meaning to 'cosmic Word', but with an additional, more sublime quality.

World-Spirit (Weltengeist) v. 24: this term appears to refer to the Spirit of the Earth, (meaning the cosmic Christ) but includes other spiritual influences inherent to the Earth's soul; these may have their origin in the planetary spheres.

Agape: Love which is selfless and lives not only in one's feelings but in the core of one's will.

See the author's website for a list of
his other books:

www.rudolfsteinerstudies.com

www.ingramcontent.com/pod-product-compliance
Lightning Source LLC
Chambersburg PA
CBHW071801090426
42737CB00012B/1909